THE
Amazing
BRAIN

Addiction

By
Susan Papa

Scientific Consultant:
Dr. Paul Thompson
Assistant Professor of Neurology, UCLA

BLACKBIRCH PRESS, INC.
WOODBRIDGE, CONNECTICUT

Published by Blackbirch Press, Inc.
260 Amity Road
Woodbridge, CT 06525
Web site: http://www.blackbirch.com
e-mail: staff@blackbirch.com
© 2001 Blackbirch Press, Inc.

Printed in Belgium

10 9 8 7 6 5 4 3 2 1

Photo credits:
Cover, back cover, pages 4-5, 11 (top left and bottom), 12-13, 18-20, 24,
34-35 (top), 36-37 (bottom), 40, 46-47, 49, 56, 59: PhotoDisc; pages 8-9,
11 (top right), 16, 30, 37 (top), 43, 50, 52-54, 57-58: Blackbirch Press;
pages 17, 29, 33, 44-45: LifeArt; page 35 (bottom): Corel Corporation.

Library of Congress Cataloging-in-Publication Data

Papa, Susan.
Addiction / by Susan Papa.
        p. cm. — (The amazing brain)
Includes index.
        ISBN 1-56711-421-0 (hardcover)
1. Substance abuse—Pathophysiology—Juvenile literature. 2. Brain—Effect
of drugs on—Juvenile literature. 3. Drug abuse—Juvenile literature. [1.
Brian—Effect of drugs on. 2. Drug abuse.] I. Title. II. Amazing brain
series.

RC564.3 .M556 2001   00-011948
616.86—dc21

Table of Contents

Chapter 1

What Is Addiction?

Lincoln School Library

"**J**ust one more and that's the last one, I promise. I can stop whenever I want."

Have you ever heard anyone say this? You may have heard these words from a friend, one of your parents, or even from yourself. What was the "one more" that the person was speaking of? A drink? A pill? A cigarette? A cup of coffee?

Unfortunately, someone who boasts that "I can stop whenever I want" is often struggling unsuccessfully against a dangerous habit. This person may be an addict.

What Is Addiction?

Addiction is a tricky topic. Definitions of addiction, and attitudes toward it, have shifted dramatically over time. Most people have their own ideas, attitudes, and opinions about addiction. These feelings are based on personal beliefs, experiences with friends and family, or interest in the troubled lives of famous athletes, musicians, or actors. Despite recent great

Most people mistake obsessions or compulsive behavior with true addictions.

advances in research and understanding, controversy remains over exactly what addiction is. Scientists and researchers disagree over the guidelines for judging addiction, and many have differing views on the best ways to combat and treat addiction. They even disagree on which substances or activities are technically addictive.

In this book, we will talk about addiction as it relates specifically to drugs or other substances. We will focus most of the discussion on the potentially harmful effects these substances can have with long-term use. Other activities—such as over-use of the Internet, gambling, eating, or shopping—are often referred to as addictions, but they are mostly considered to be compulsive or obsessive behaviors. Overindulging in these activities may involve some of the same areas of the brain as drug addiction does, but no one has yet proven this connection.

So, just what is addiction? Let's start with the disagreement over how to define drug addiction. While nearly everyone agrees that the body's biochemistry plays a key role in addiction, experts tend to fall into two groups that disagree on just how important the biology is. The first group believes that addiction is mostly a biological disease. The second group believes that addiction is mostly a problem of learned behavior.

Addiction as a Disease

Thinking of addiction as a disease means comparing it to any illness that might overtake the body—pneumonia, cancer, chicken pox. These illnesses affect the cells of our bodies, and they need to be treated with medicines and other means. And, just as someone cannot say in the middle of the chicken pox, "I'm finished with itching; my rash will be gone by 2 o'clock!", neither can an addict simply decide to stop using drugs. Once a body has become dependent on a drug, there is an uncontrollable urge to consume it—an urge that the brain signals to the body just as it does for hunger or thirst.

Some people think that addicts are weak or stupid. Those who believe addiction is a biological disease say that an addict has lost control over his or her body, including his or her free will and self-control. The biological proponents say that addicts need medication, counseling, and complete abstinence from the addictive drug in order to recover and regain a normal life.

Addiction as a Voluntary Behavior

Though most experts agree that biology and body chemistry play some role in addiction, they disagree on exactly how much this role has been scientifically proven. Some experts deny the idea of addiction as a disease—they say that calling it a biological problem relieves addicts of responsibility for their actions. These experts feel that it is the behavior of a drug user—his or her choice to take drugs—that transforms a person into an addict. Changes in brain biochemistry, these experts say, are not the key to addiction.

According to this view, many (though not all) addicts are capable of breaking their addictions without the help of doctors, medications, or counselors, even though doing so is quite difficult.

So Which Is It?

Like many good debates, there is probably some truth to each side's beliefs about addiction—the absolute truth is difficult to know for certain. In this book, we will approach addiction primarily as a disease caused by two things: tolerance and dependence. With addiction, a person uses a drug often enough to change his or her brain chemistry. As the brain chemistry

Although most experts agree that body chemistry plays a role in addiction, personal choices and behavior are also key elements.

Seeing the Signs

It isn't always easy to recognize when someone, even yourself, is addicted. Many addicts are good at fooling themselves and others into believing they "have it all under control." There are, however, some classic signs of addiction that eventually become hard to hide:

- Using drugs even though it prevents functioning at work, school, or home
- Using drugs when it is physically endangering you or others, like drinking and driving a car
- Getting arrested, suspended from school, or fired from a job for drug-related reasons, but continuing to use drugs
- Having arguments with parents, friends, or other people about drug use
- Taking drugs to relieve stress or anxiety
- Failing classes or skipping school, work, or other commitments because of drugs
- Trying to quit drugs, but can't
- Stealing or borrowing money to buy drugs
- Behaving very differently; exhibiting sharp personality changes, including irritability, anger, paranoia, severe depression, or emotional unsteadiness.

If you, or someone you know, shows any of these behavior patterns, that person should seek help. Help can come from any number of trusted people: a parent, a doctor, a rabbi or priest, a counselor, or a friend.

changes, more and more drug is needed to produce the desired effect (tolerance). At the same time the brain is craving higher and higher doses of a drug, the brain is also thinking that it actually needs the drug to survive (dependence). In addition to changes in the brain, addiction can cause changes in other parts of the body, such as the liver, lungs, or heart. These changes can make it even harder for an addict to quit.

Addiction causes more than physical changes in an addict. It can also cause psychological changes. Because the brain's chemistry is being altered, addiction often causes serious shifts in personality. Addicts often become paranoid, highly emotional, aggressive, even homicidal or suicidal. For most true addicts, their addiction becomes the center of everything in their lives. Their need for a drug becomes so strong that it occupies their every thought and motivates their every action. An addict often feels stuck in a perpetual state of discomfort—he or she is trapped inside a body that can never get enough of what it craves.

Who Can Become an Addict?

Addiction knows no boundaries. Any kind of person can become an addict. There are rich addicts, poor addicts, educated addicts, young and old addicts. All human beings have the potential to become addicted because all humans have brains that basically work the same way. Addictive drugs often affect aspects of brain function that oversee fulfillment of some of our most basic needs. These parts exist in every human brain. So, it's fair to say that if you have a brain, you have the potential to become addicted.

Remember that addicts can be found in all walks of life, from street criminals to police officers, from dropouts to professors, from distant relatives to people in your immediate family. Whether you realize it or not, you probably know at least one addicted person.

It seems logical to say that behavior plays a very large role in propelling a drug user down the path toward addiction. Just as any drug user has the potential to become an addict, any drug user also has the potential not to become an addict. By making good decisions from the outset, and exerting will power early on, many people can defy addiction before the drug takes over. Of course, the best way to be sure to avoid addiction is never to use a drug in the first place.

People of all ages and walks of life can become addicted.

Addictive Drugs

The Paradox of Drugs

Drugs. You hear this word all the time. Newspaper headlines constantly feature stories about the ongoing "War on Drugs." Famous athletes and actors in public-service commercials encourage you to think about your future and "just say no" to harmful drugs. There's a constant barrage of messages that discourages the use of drugs. But there are also a lot of mixed messages about drugs in our society. Some potentially addictive drugs—such as alcohol, caffeine, and tobacco—are legal. Other drugs—such as pain relievers, cold remedies, and allergy medicines—are a common part of our everyday lives. Still others—prescription only—are prescribed and used regularly. For many people, prescription drugs are as common each day as non-prescription drugs.

Because of its many forms and uses, the word "drug" has many meanings. It can refer to illegal substances, such as marijuana, cocaine, or heroin; it can refer to the medicines your doctor prescribes to help you get through an illness; it can refer to the aspirin and cough syrup you take when you have a bad cold.

Drugs are not only widespread, both legal and illegal, they can also be both good and bad for you. Drugs represent great medical advances for society, and at the same time they can create terrible social and personal problems. The world of drugs is a paradoxical one; it is full of contradictions.

Psychoactive Drugs

Drugs of all kinds act on the body to change it in some way. Usually, the change is only temporary. Some drugs are intended for use as medicines, to help cure, treat, or prevent illness—vaccines prevent certain diseases, antibiotics fight infections, aspirin relieves aches and pains.

To most people, the word *drugs* means illegal "substances," such as cocaine, LSD, amphetamines ("speed"), crystal meth, and others. What do these drugs do? Most of them change how the user thinks, feels, and acts by changing the way the user's brain actually functions. Drugs that change brain function are also called psychoactive drugs. The Greek word for "mind" is *psyche*, and the Latin root for "do" is *act-*; psychoactive drugs "do something to our brains." Psychoactive drugs can be very alluring. Often, the effect they have on the brain provides the user with a heightened sense of well-being, energy, or confidence. But these effects are only temporary. And the side effects of those pleasurable feelings can be dangerous.

Not all psychoactive drugs are illegal. Some medicines used to treat mental illness are psychoactive.

Average Caffeine Content of Selected Foods, Drinks, and Over-the-Counter Medications

If you're like most people, you know that coffee and tea contain caffeine. But did you know that most sodas, most chocolate products, and many aspirin and cold remedies contain some level of caffeine? Here is a partial list of some common everyday products and their caffeine levels. (Caffeine content is per 8 oz. for drinks, and per 1 pill for medications.)

No-Doz medicine, extra strength	200 mg
Vivarin	200 mg
Coffee, brewed	85–130 mg
Excedrin pain reliever	65 mg
Tea, brewed	40–60 mg
Jolt cola	47.3 mg
Mountain Dew, regular or diet	37 mg
Surge	35 mg
Anacin pain reliever	32 mg
Midol pain reliever	32 mg
Coca-Cola, regular or diet	31 mg

Non-drowsy cold relief tablet	30 mg
Tea, iced	25 mg
Pepsi	25 mg
Diet Pepsi	24 mg
Semi-sweet dark chocolate, 1 oz.	20–35 mg
Coffee ice cream, 8 oz.	20 mg
Barq's root beer, regular	15 mg
Milk chocolate, 1 oz.	6–15 mg
Cocoa/chocolate milk	5–6 mg
Coffee, decaffeinated, brewed	3 mg

Sources:
www.thecocacolacompany.com,
www. pepsi.com,
www.webmd.com,
www.batnet.com/spencer,
www. excedrin.com

Poppy plants are the source of heroin.

Drugs of Abuse

The U.S. Drug Enforcement Administration lists six groups of illegal substances, or drugs, that can be "abused," that is, used inappropriately and/or dangerously. Five of the six categories are psychoactive drugs. The categories are:

- *Narcotics*, which includes heroin, codeine, and morphine
- *Depressants*, which includes sedatives and tranquilizers
- *Stimulants*, which includes cocaine, amphetamines, and Ritalin
- *Hallucinogens*, which includes LSD and mescaline
- *Cannabis*, which includes marijuana and hashish
- *Steroids*, of which there are many varieties, some legal and some illegal.

While you have probably heard a lot about steroids as a drug that is commonly misused by athletes, this category of drugs will not be discussed here. Steroids do not work instantly on the

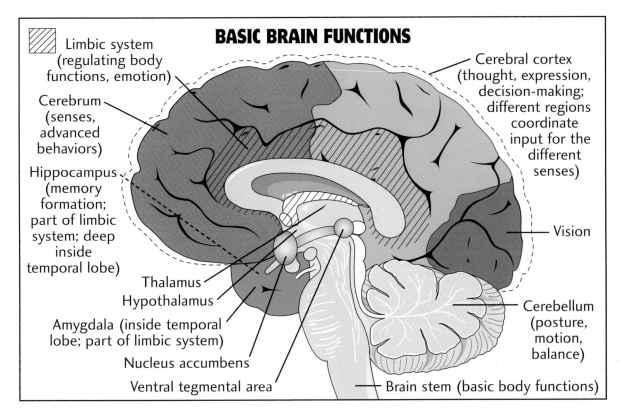

BASIC BRAIN FUNCTIONS

Limbic system (regulating body functions, emotion)

Cerebrum (senses, advanced behaviors)

Hippocampus (memory formation; part of limbic system; deep inside temporal lobe)

Thalamus

Hypothalamus

Amygdala (inside temporal lobe; part of limbic system)

Nucleus accumbens

Ventral tegmental area

Cerebral cortex (thought, expression, decision-making; different regions coordinate input for the different senses)

Vision

Cerebellum (posture, motion, balance)

Brain stem (basic body functions)

brain; instead their main effects are on the muscles and other parts of the body.

Legal Psychoactive Drugs

To make the U.S. Drug Enforcement Administration's list, a drug must be illegal, psychoactive, and have the potential to be abused. There are, however, a number of drugs that are not illegal, but are psychoactive and potentially abused. Alcohol and nicotine (found in tobacco) are the two most commonly used—and abused—drugs in the world. They are also used more widely than any illegal substances. Alcohol is a depressant—when abused, it impairs motor function (including balance, speech, coordination, and vision), judgment, and can cause mild to severe shifts in personality. Nicotine is a highly addictive stimulant. It activates the brain circuitry that regulates feelings of pleasure. Many inhalants (vapors that are breathed in) can be obtained legally as well, but their unintended use as hallucinogenic (hallucination-producing) and depressant drugs is abusive and extremely dangerous. Caffeine, found naturally in coffee, tea, cola nuts, mate, guarana, and chocolate, is probably the most popular drug in the world. While legal and relatively safe when used in moderation, caffeine is nonetheless an addictive stimulant that can be dangerous if abused. Among its effects are stimulation of the central nervous system, the cardiac (heart) muscles, and the respiratory (breathing) system. If taken in excessive quantities (250 mg or more) caffeine can produce severe muscle twitching, nervousness, insomnia, irregular heartbeat, and many other "nervous disorders." Some studies have linked consumption of high levels of caffeine to cancer and heart disease.

Cigarettes, alcohol, and caffeine are the most widely used addictive drugs in the world.

The Ultimate "Drug Delivery System"

Cigarette smoking is by far the most widespread form of nicotine addiction in the United States. An estimated 65 million Americans are regular smokers, and another 7 million Americans are regular users of smokeless tobacco.

It is estimated that, each day in the United States, nearly 3,000 people under the age of 18 will start smoking.

The average cigarette sold on the U.S. market contains 10 milligrams or more of nicotine. Through inhaling the smoke, the average smoker takes in about 1 to 2 milligrams of nicotine per cigarette. The drug is absorbed through the skin and mucous lining of the mouth and nose, as well as by inhalation in the lungs.

The National Institute on Drug Abuse calls the cigarette "a very efficient and highly engineered drug delivery system." By inhaling smoke while smoking, the brain receives the nicotine within 10 seconds. The peak effects of the drug wear off quickly, however, which causes the smoker to continue "dosing" throughout the day to maintain the pleasurable effects and avoid symptoms of withdrawal. Even while the cigarette is lit, the smoker takes an average of 10 puffs over an average period of 5 minutes. That means a person who smokes an average of 30 cigarettes per day gets 300 daily "hits" of nicotine. This habit of constant dosing is an important factor in nicotine's highly addictive nature.

Recent research indicates that nicotine may not be the only psychoactive ingredient in tobacco (the smoke of which contains more than 4,000 chemicals). Studies show a marked decrease in the levels of an enzyme called MAO in smokers—an enzyme that breaks down the neurotransmitter dopamine in the brain (dopamine is involved in regulating the desire to take drugs). Scientists believe that some chemical other than nicotine helps to keep a smoker's dopamine levels high, thus resulting in a stronger continuous desire for repeated drug use.

Communication in the Brain

It's All in Your Head

To understand how addictive substances truly work, you have to look inside your head—or someone else's head. Brain cells communicate with one another and with other body parts by using electrochemical signals. These electrochemical signals travel along pathways—the body's electrical "wiring"— called neurons, which make up the body's nerves. Scientists have found that the chemicals in various drugs affect different parts of the brain, each interfering or altering the normal ways in which brain cells communicate.

Chemical Messages

Billions of cells make up the brain. Most (about 90 percent) are glia, a kind of helper or support cell. The glia assist the remaining 10 percent of brain cells, which are nerve cells, also called neurons. Neurons communicate with one another constantly through chemical signals that carry messages throughout the brain. Neurons are also found throughout the body—they are always carrying messages back and forth between the brain and places such as the stomach or little finger. Most messages between the brain and the body travel at least partway along the spinal cord, the bundle of neurons encased in the protective bones of the spine in the middle of your back. If you thought of the nerve pathways of your body as transportation routes of increasing size and capacity, the smallest nerves would be the "footpaths" and the "back roads." As the nerves got closer to the spinal cord, the pathways would widen into routes and parkways. The spinal cord would be the six-lane superhighway. The combination of the brain, spinal cord, and other neurons makes up the body's nervous system.

The nervous system oversees all of the body's functioning. It regulates basic impulses—such as increasing breath to run from danger—but it also controls complicated activities, such as learning a foreign language or solving a brainteaser. Researchers used to think that signals passed from one nerve cell to another by electrical impulses, but it is now known that, while electricity plays a role within the neuron itself, chemicals called neurotransmitters travel across the spaces between neurons.

The Neuron

Every neuron has a cell body and extensions at either end, called the dendrites and axons. Dendrites bring information to the cell body, and axons take information away from it. A neuron looks a bit like a tree, with branches, a trunk, and roots. Incoming messages (chemical signals from neurotransmitters) are received by the dendrites, which are the spreading tree branches. Once inside the neuron, the messages create an electrical signal as well, which helps them travel from the dendrites to the cell body. The electrochemical messages continue to the other end of the nerve cell, the axon, which looks first like the trunk and then like the roots of a tree. The axon then passes the message, now a chemical signal only again, to the dendrites of the next neuron by jumping across the gap between the two neurons, called the synaptic cleft. When a neuron completes this cycle of receiving and sending a message, it has "fired."

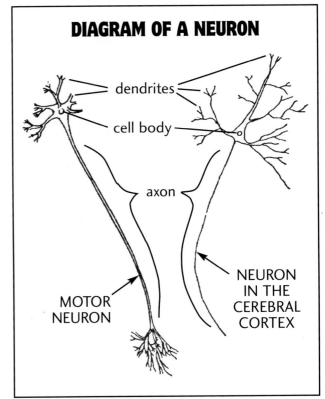

DIAGRAM OF A NEURON

dendrites

cell body

axon

MOTOR NEURON

NEURON IN THE CEREBRAL CORTEX

Each nerve cell receives messages from many other nerve cells around it. Likewise, the chemical signals of each neuron travel to many other neurons as well. One neuron can have several axons, although most have only one. In humans, axons can be extremely short or extend up to 4 feet—in a giraffe, they're up to 15 feet! At the end of each axon may be thousands of tiny "roots," each of which can contact another neuron. In addition, a neuron can have more than 10,000 dendrites, each of which can receive chemical messages from other neurons.

Neurotransmitters and Synapses

Neurons do not touch each other. They do, however, have an important meeting point where their messages are passed. This meeting place is called the synapse, and it consists of the tips of the axon of one neuron, the tips of the dendrites of another neuron, and a tiny fluid-filled gap called the synaptic cleft, in

Can Science Combat Addiction?

Several recent studies on possible genetic causes of addiction may point scientists in a new direction. These studies suggest that some people are born with an abnormality in the gene that directs growth of neural receptors for the neurotransmitter dopamine. Dopamine is essential in the pleasure pathway, so people whose brains are less able to

Recent research suggests a possible connection between addiction and low levels of dopamine in the brain.

receive and utilize dopamine may experience "life with less joy," says Dr. Ernest P. Noble, professor of psychiatry and biobehavioral sciences at the University of California at Los Angeles. Many of these same people have reported that the first time they felt "fully alive" was after trying their first drink or illegal drug.

Researchers at the Brookhaven National Laboratory in New York tested people who had never used illegal drugs. After scanning their brains to estimate how many dopamine receptors each person had, the researchers injected the subjects with a small amount of the stimulant Ritalin, commonly used to treat attention deficit disorder (ADD). The results showed two clear groups: the group with low numbers of dopamine receptors liked the way the Ritalin made them feel; the group with high numbers of receptors found the drug quite unpleasant.

So can adding dopamine receptors help to combat drug abuse? The early results are promising. Dr. Panayotis Thanos of Brookhaven used gene therapy to increase the number of dopamine receptors in rats that had learned to use alcohol. After the boost, the rats actually stopped choosing to drink.

between the two neurons. Neurotransmitters flow from the axons across the synaptic clefts, entering slots on the dendrites of the receiving neurons. Each slot is called a receptor, and each receptor is extremely specific. Think of the neurotransmitter as a key, and the receptor as a lock. Just as a lock will accept only a certain key, any one receptor usually has only one neurotransmitter that it can receive.

Once attached to a dendrite, a neurotransmitter triggers electrical signals that result in one of two events: either the message is passed to the next neuron in the communication line, which then fires, or the message is prevented from being forwarded. Neurotransmitters that cause the next neuron to fire are excitatory; neurotransmitters that prevent the next neuron from firing are inhibitory.

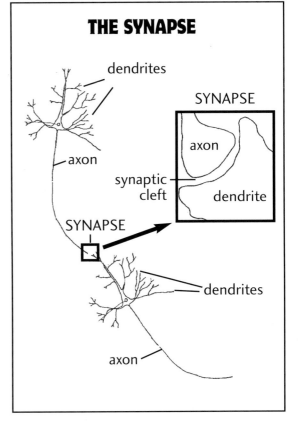

Synapses are the meeting places for neurons, where neurotransmitters are released by the axons of one neuron to cross the synaptic cleft and "dock" in the dendrites of another neuron.

What happens to a "used" neurotransmitter after it has done its specific job of swimming across the synaptic cleft and fitting itself into the receptor? Most often, the body recycles it, and the neuron that released the neurotransmitter reabsorbs it for use another time. This is called re-uptake. Sometimes, the used neurotransmitter is destroyed; other times, it is absorbed by the helper glia cells.

Drugs and the Brain's Function

How do drugs interact with the brain's communication system? Your billions of neurons use more than 150 different known neurotransmitter chemicals. Every thought ("I'm hungry"), or action (Let's get out of here!'), or feeling ("I love you") depends on your brain's neurons and the chemical signals that they send and receive. Anything that interferes with the transmission of messages between neurons affects your body and your mind.

"I Need" vs. "I Think"

Think of the brain, in a very simplified way, as having two distinct regions—Need and Thought. In the Need region are our basic instincts that make us act for pleasure, comfort, and survival. Urges for food and drink, sleep, and companionship are found here. In terms of human evolution, Need is older, located deep within the brain. A very similar Need-like area exists in all animals. The major organ of the brain that regulates Need is the hypothalamus (see page 17). It is located near the front of the brain, but deep within its central core.

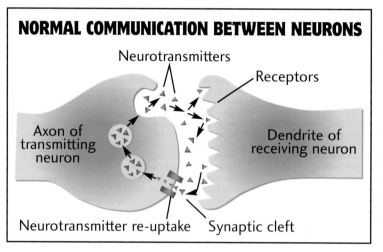

NORMAL COMMUNICATION BETWEEN NEURONS

Neurotransmitters

Receptors

Axon of transmitting neuron

Dendrite of receiving neuron

Neurotransmitter re-uptake   Synaptic cleft

The other region, Thought, is a place of reflection and ideas about ourselves in relation to the outside world. This is where learning, understanding, analyzing, and organizing new information occurs, as well as decision making. The Thought region is much larger in humans than in other animals. It represents the special ability that humans have developed to think and act based on reason and judgment. The part of the brain that is primarily responsible for thought and understanding is the cerebral cortex. This area is a thin, deeply wrinkled layer that covers most of the outer brain and lies directly under the skull (see page 17).

Both the Need and Thought areas of the brain are extremely important, and each needs the other for a human being to function properly.

The "Pleasure Pathway"

Where in the brain would you expect something called the "pleasure pathway" to be: Need, or Thought? It seems to be mostly in the Need region, deep in the brain, near the hypothalamus. The pleasure pathway is a network of neurons that brings about good feelings in response to pleasurable activities: eating your favorite food, dancing with someone you love, sitting in front of a warm fire on a snowy day, or falling asleep in a safe place.

Every time you learn something, your neurons make new connections—the wiring in your brain is physically changed, and new "pathways," or patterns of communication, are formed. Part of the function of the pleasure pathway is helping your brain keep track of the positive experiences and feelings you have learned. The pleasure pathway then helps influence your behavior by urging you to repeat what makes you feel good. Impulses from the pleasure pathway can be hard to resist. In some people, the urge to repeat a pleasurable experience is nearly impossible to deny.

Scientists have not yet mapped all the organs of the brain that are linked to the pleasure pathway, but three of the most important organs (or groups of organs) are certain. One is the limbic system, which is partly responsible for emotion and memory. The limbic system is formed by a group of small structures, two of which—the amygdala and the nucleus accumbens (which works with the ventral tegmental area)—seem especially important in the experience and memory of pleasure. The second organ is the brain stem, which is the most primitive, ancient part of the brain. The brain stem is partially surrounded by the limbic system. The third organ involved in pleasure is the hypothalamus—which also controls the Need regions of the brain. Although it is no bigger than the tip of your thumb, the hypothalamus is essential for our survival. It is the "command center" for body temperature, thirst and appetite, sexual behavior, blood pressure, aggression, fear, sleep, and more.

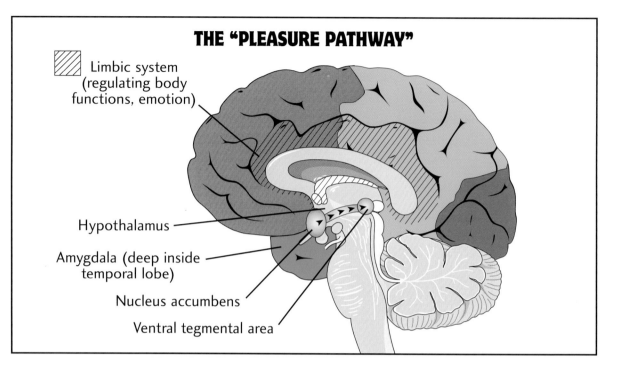

THE "PLEASURE PATHWAY"

Limbic system (regulating body functions, emotion)

Hypothalamus

Amygdala (deep inside temporal lobe)

Nucleus accumbens

Ventral tegmental area

Gotta Have It

Most scientific research has shown that many of the most significant addictive drug–induced changes in the brain occur in the pleasure pathway. In 1954, Olds and Milner performed a groundbreaking experiment on the brain and the workings of the pleasure pathway. A rat with an electrode (an electrical conductor) in its brain was made to feel a mild shock when it entered one corner of its cage. The researchers hypothesized that the stimulation would be unpleasant for the rat and, consequently, the animal would learn to avoid that part of the cage.

As sometimes happens in science, an accident helped to change the course of brain research. The electrode in the rat's brain ended up in an unintended location—in the limbic system, near the hypothalamus. Instead of causing pain, the electric impulses were stimulating some of the "pleasure centers" of the brain. As a result, instead of avoiding the electrical stimulus, the rats kept coming back for more!

Many related experiments followed. In one, rats could press a bar to obtain electrical stimulation in the limbic system and hypothalamus, now proved to be part of the pleasure pathway. Before too long, the sensation became more important than anything else to the rats. The urge for pleasure made them abandon their normal behavior. They chose not to eat or drink rather than leave the bar behind. They pushed it thousands of times in a row until they fell dead asleep from exhaustion. Then, after a brief rest, they would return directly to pushing the bar as eagerly as before.

Drugs and the Pleasure Pathway

As you have perhaps guessed, it's not just electrodes that can stimulate the pleasure pathway—psychoactive drugs can also have this effect. The fact that the rats in the experiments chose to skip eating and drinking is extremely important. They left behind the essential everyday activities that provide animals—including humans—with the ability to thrive and be healthy.

In other pleasure pathway experiments, pigeons, monkeys, and rats will work to press a lever that results in a drug injection; they consistently choose this lever over one that results in food. The drugs for which the animals will work hardest are the same drugs considered the most addictive in humans: cocaine, amphetamines, heroin, and alcohol, among others. Researchers have also found that, if the pleasure pathway in an animal is damaged, it will not be overcome by the need to get drugs. Clearly, the process of addiction is closely linked to the functioning of the neural circuit called the pleasure pathway.

Human drug addicts—just like the animals in the laboratory experiments—will forsake the normal needs and pleasures of daily life, such as food, drink, and social interaction, in favor of an addictive drug. Once an addiction has taken firm hold of the brain and body, nothing but the drug seems to matter to the addict.

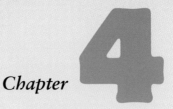

Chapter

Drugs and the Brain

How Drugs Work

Imagine a visitor ringing your front doorbell. One or two short rings announces that you have a guest, an important piece of information. But what if you can't get to the door quickly and the visitor gets impatient, holding the button down continuously? The constant sound is no longer informative; you already know someone is there. Instead, it is a terrible irritation.

Drugs have a parallel effect on your brain. Normally, a neurotransmitter passes between two neurons just long enough to send information. Drugs extend that chemical signal longer than it should last. While the constantly ringing doorbell would probably drive you crazy, a drug's extended chemical message can be perceived by your brain as pleasurable. However, the abnormal signals may be harmful to the body. They may cause changes in the way the nervous system functions—specifically interfering with the way we sense, interpret, and respond to the world around us. If you consider how much you rely upon your senses to help you react to the world around you, you will realize that this kind of sensory interference can be very dangerous.

Tampering with the Nervous System

The brain is the center of our nervous system, the network of neurons that allows the brain and the body to communicate and react to the environment. The nervous system has two main parts. The central nervous system includes the brain and spinal cord, which act as the body's control center. The peripheral nervous system includes all other nerves, whose neurons connect the brain and spinal cord to muscles and glands. Changes in the way that this network functions affect more than just the brain; they can alter sensation or function of anything from hands and feet to internal organs such as the heart and lungs.

The first job of the nervous system is to sense changes. For example, you are driving on a dark, rainy night when you see something large dart out into the road. Within a fraction of a second, you realize it is a deer, frozen in your headlights. You are not aware of it, but your brain and body have already responded to the potential emergency. Your adrenal gland has released a dose of epinephrine. This makes your heart rate increase. Your breathing is faster. Your eyes are open wide. Without thinking, you slam on the brakes, skidding to a stop and avoiding the deer by a few inches.

When the nervous system detects a change, its second function is activated: perception. The brain interprets and explains the changes. You not only recognize that something is in your way in the road, you also realize that the thing is a deer. Then you realize that this poses a potentially serious danger.

The third function of your nervous system is to respond. Sensing "emergency," your brain sends out its alarm to all needed parts of your body, enabling you to react almost instantly. The adrenaline is a stimulant designed to give the body a burst of extra energy and power in situations where the brain believes survival is at stake. Your foot jams on the brake pedal. The car stops in time and you—and the deer—are saved.

These three kinds of nervous system functions—sensing, perceiving, and reacting—happen instantaneously every minute of the day in varying degrees. In most cases, we are not even aware that such processes are underway. When drugs are added to the system, the normal speed and process of sensing, perceiving, and responding is changed. Sometimes the speed is increased, sometimes it is slowed down dramatically. Either way, the consequences are potentially dangerous. Consider alcohol for a moment. As a depressant, alcohol slows the nervous system processes of sensing, perceiving, and reacting. Now consider the same driving scenario with the deer. What happens if there is a delay in your ability to sense

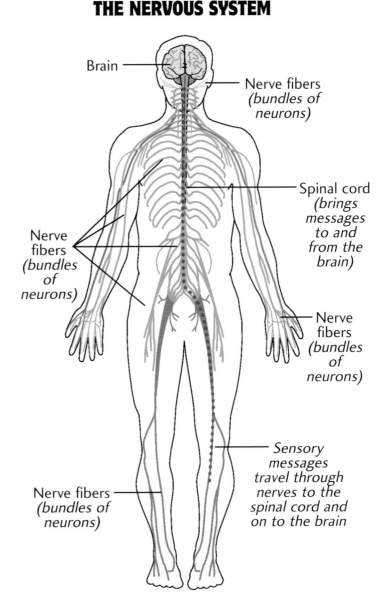

THE NERVOUS SYSTEM

Brain

Nerve fibers
(bundles of neurons)

Spinal cord
(brings messages to and from the brain)

Nerve fibers
(bundles of neurons)

Nerve fibers
(bundles of neurons)

Sensory messages travel through nerves to the spinal cord and on to the brain

Nerve fibers
(bundles of neurons)

Depressants, such as alcohol, impair the senses by slowing the processes of perceiving and reacting.

that a deer has jumped into the road? And what if your brain's alarm takes a little longer to send its message to your heart, lungs, eyes, and foot? And what if your foot is delayed just a fraction of a second before it reaches for the brake pedal?

Getting to the Brain

How do chemicals get to the brain in the first place? In order for a drug to affect your body, it must reach the neurons. The only route to the neurons is through the blood, which is carried by the circulatory system. There are a variety of ways to get a drug into the blood.

When a drug is swallowed, it enters the circulatory system through the lining of the stomach and intestines. Though this is probably the most common way drugs are absorbed, it is also the slowest and least efficient way to get a drug to the brain.

Does the Body Manufacture Its Own Drugs?

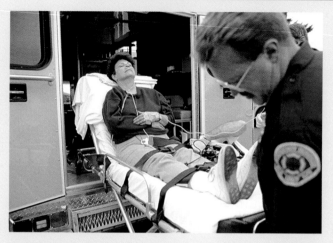

Most drugs act indirectly on neural receptors; they influence neurons, which then release neurotransmitters to their receptors. In 1973, Drs. Candace Pert and Solomon Snyder made the breakthrough discovery that opiates—narcotic drugs such as morphine—eliminated the neurotransmitter "middleman" by fitting themselves directly into the brain's neural receptors!

Since receptors are like locks whose only keys are neurotransmitters, scientists hypothesized that opiates must resemble some neurotransmitter enough to fool that neurotransmitter's receptor into accepting the drug instead of the body's own chemical. Later research proved this to be true: the body does make its own neurotransmitter opiates, called the endorphins (short for endogenous morphine, meaning "morphine within") and enkephalins ("inside the head"). The endorphin/enkephalin family, as it is called, is the body's natural pain-control system. These neurotransmitters are released when the body undergoes intense stress or harm.

After long periods of physical exercise, endorphins are also believed to cause the euphoria known as "runner's high." Why? The body is probably responding to what it interprets as danger (the physical stress or, perhaps, the actual pain of extended exercise). To help you keep going (and escape the "danger"), the body activates its own natural pain-relief system.

Much of the drug is lost to the digestive system's natural defenses, which are partly designed to "weed out" useful nutrients from waste products or harmful substances. The speed with which a drug gets into the blood this way also depends on whether the stomach has food in it—food slows down absorption. Long-term use of drugs that travel through the digestive system can damage any organ along the way. People who abuse alcohol, for example, often develop liver disease, because it is the liver's job to remove dangerous substances from the blood.

Because the stomach is a relatively inefficient region for drug absorption, drug abusers and addicts usually use other methods. Mucous tissues in the mouth and nose, where skin surfaces are thinner and more delicate and blood vessels are very close to the skin, absorb chemicals relatively quickly. Tobacco and cocaine are two drugs commonly absorbed through the mouth and nose. Another swift route into the circulatory system is by way of the lungs. This is the absorption method used by people who smoke. Large doses of nicotine from cigarettes, THC from marijuana, or

Psychoactive drugs affect the levels of dopamine in the brain, which affects mood and feeling.

cocaine from crack can travel from the lining of the lungs to the brain in seconds. In addition to the risks of the drugs themselves, people who take drugs these ways also run the risk of cancers of the mouth, nose, throat, and lungs.

The fastest—and most dangerous—way to get a drug into the circulatory system is to inject it directly with a needle and syringe. Drugs injected into the bloodstream stop at the heart before they ever get to the brain. This alone may cause instant death. There are also the health risks of dirty needles and risks of not injecting properly (if air gets into the veins, it can cause death). Another great danger of injected drugs, such as heroin, is that the entire dose enters the circulatory system at once, making it easy to take too much. Overdoses affect neurotransmitters very rapidly, and they can overwhelm the brain and shut down essential body functions—like breathing.

Once a drug enters the circulatory system, and is brought by the blood to the brain, it begins to affect various areas of the nervous system, including the pleasure pathway.

The Chemistry of the Pleasure Pathway

Psychoactive drugs change the way that the pleasure pathway's neurons use neurotransmitters. Many neurotransmitters become active when drugs enter the brain. Dopamine, in particular, seems to be the chief chemical messenger (neurotransmitter) in the pleasure pathway.

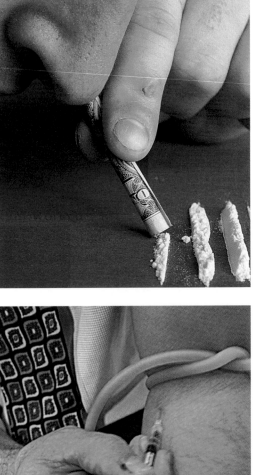

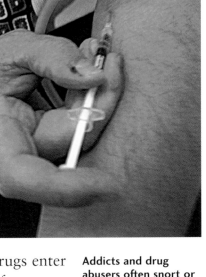

Addicts and drug abusers often snort or inject a drug for a quicker effect.

Neurons are at work all the time—there is a constant flow of neurotransmitters at synapses. In the case of dopamine, this flow may be a built-in part of your mood. When you feel really good, the dopamine flow increases. In fact, some brain researchers believe that depression may be related to a shortage of dopamine. Irregularities in dopamine levels and dopamine receptors also seem to be common in the brains of drug users.

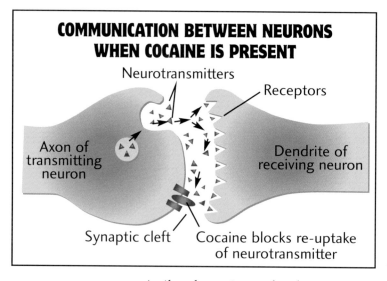

COMMUNICATION BETWEEN NEURONS WHEN COCAINE IS PRESENT

Neurotransmitters

Receptors

Axon of transmitting neuron

Dendrite of receiving neuron

Synaptic cleft

Cocaine blocks re-uptake of neurotransmitter

Some drugs, such as heroin and amphetamines, cause the brain to produce more dopamine. This creates a sudden increase in the signals to neural receptors, particularly in the pleasure pathway. Remember the doorbell example at the beginning of this chapter? Imagine that the doorbell suddenly sounded as loud as a jet plane. That's what the effect of heroin and similar drugs is on the dopamine receptors. Other drugs, like cocaine, interfere with the re-uptake systems that remove dopamine after a message has been sent. This prevents the signals to the receptors from stopping after the message is delivered—not unlike the person who won't take his finger off your doorbell, even after you've answered the door. Nicotine affects dopamine at both ends; it causes dopamine production to increase and, at the same time, its slows dopamine re-uptake. The brain is tricked into perceiving the unusually high exposure to dopamine in the pleasure pathway as a good thing, even though the effects on your body and mind may be dangerous. Because your brain equates its perception of "good thing" with "get as much of the good thing as possible," nicotine and its effects are extremely addictive.

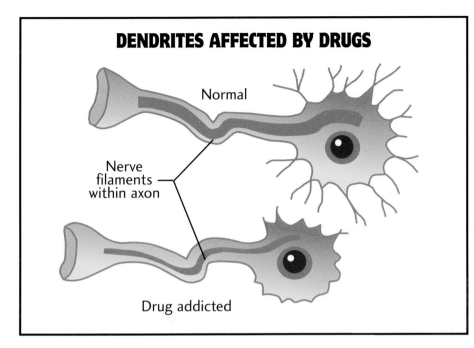

DENDRITES AFFECTED BY DRUGS

Normal

Nerve filaments within axon

Drug addicted

Addiction causes the shape of nerve cells to change, sometimes permanently.

Addiction Takes Time

Addiction causes the structure of synapses and the shape of nerve cells to change. With repeated use—addictive use—many drugs will permanently change the structure of neurons. This physical change alters the way neurons communicate with each other. Because networks of nerve cells (made of neurons) control the operation of the brain—which in turn controls feelings, behavior, and responses to the world—any change in neurons means both the body and the mind will change as a result.

In most cases, addiction does not happen overnight. These changes take time and require repeated consumption of a drug. Almost no one becomes addicted the first time he or she smokes a cigarette, takes a drink of alcohol, or consumes a cup of coffee. Researchers do believe, however, that some people are more biologically susceptible to becoming addicted than others. Depending on the specifics of each person's body, addiction to substances may progress very differently.

Drugs and Their Effects

We have discussed what addiction means, how neurons work, how drugs act upon the brain, which parts of the brain seem active in addiction, and the role of the neurotransmitter dopamine and the pleasure pathway. Each specific drug, however, has its own unique effect on neurotransmitters, the brain, and the body. Let's turn now to the effects of some of the best-known addictive drugs.

Alcohol

Alcohol is a sedative; that is, it slows down activity in the synapses of the brain's neurons, which reduces anxiety and provides a more "relaxed" feeling. In particular, alcohol seems to affect neurons with receptors for the neurotransmitters GABA (gamma-aminobutyric acid) and glutamate. The GABA neurons relate to the release of dopamine in the pleasure pathway, and the glutamate receptors seem to be important in the formation of new memories.

Though alcohol is a sedative, many people feel energized when they drink it—at least at first. Scientists still don't know exactly why alcohol produces this paradoxical effect, though one theory is that alcohol may be slowing down neurons whose job it is to inhibit other neurons. Just as two negatives make a positive, the result may be more brain activity, rather than less.

Long-term, heavy drinking damages the brain, liver, and digestive system. The brains of people who abuse alcohol actually shrink, and the loss seems to be largely in the number of neurons in their brains, not the helper cell glia. As you might guess, alcoholics have problems with memory, abstract thinking, problem solving, attention, and concentration. Heavy drinkers who quit will regain at least some of their mental abilities and brain size, but some of the mental deficits may be permanent.

Caffeine

Caffeine is a stimulant that increases activity in the nervous system, which causes a feeling of well-being and energy. Caffeine also stimulates the heart, kidneys, and digestive and respiratory systems. In the brain, caffeine acts primarily on neurons with receptors for adenosine. Adenosine is an inhibitory neurotransmitter that slows brain activity, but caffeine inhibits the ability of adenosine to do its job. Thus, brain activity increases with caffeine.

People who consume caffeine can develop tolerance and dependence. They can also suffer from withdrawal symptoms, which include headache, irritability, and fatigue. While these people are physically addicted, it is important to distinguish between addiction to a highly addictive and destructive psychoactive drug that can ruin your life (crack, heroin, amphetamines), and addiction to a less dangerous and more easily controlled psychoactive drug, like caffeine.

Cocaine

Cocaine is a stimulant that gives users energy, alertness, and a sense of well-being and power. In many cases, these feelings can be overwhelming and intense. Cocaine can make a person unusually talkative and physically active. It also increases the heart rate, blood pressure, and body temperature dramatically.

Cocaine works in the brain to increase the levels of the neuro-transmitters norepinephrine, epinephrine, dopamine, and serotonin in synapses. It does this by preventing their re-uptake after they go to work in their receptors. Norepinephrine and epinephrine normally prepare the body and mind for emergencies or stress— they increase alertness to the environment, raise the heart rate, send energy to muscles, and prepare the body for increased breathing. Dopamine, as we know, is essential to activating the pleasure pathway and its sensations. Serotonin is important to mood and sleep, as well as appetite and body temperature.

Caffeine is a stimulant that increases activity in the nervous system.

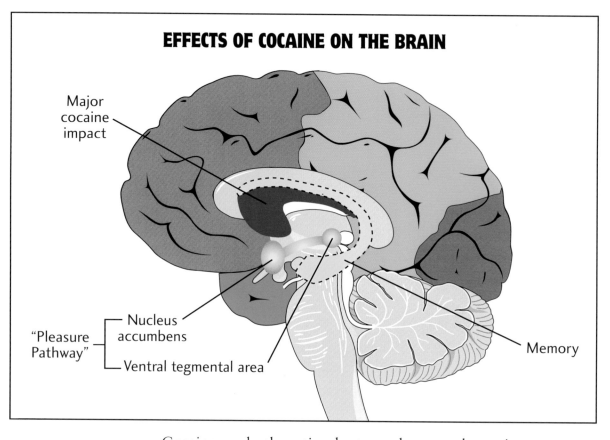

EFFECTS OF COCAINE ON THE BRAIN

Major cocaine impact

"Pleasure Pathway"
- Nucleus accumbens
- Ventral tegmental area

Memory

Cocaine, and other stimulants, such as amphetamines, are probably the most addictive drugs known. They have an extremely strong impact on the dopamine neurons of the brain, and thus create an almost irresistible drive in the user to maintain heightened dopamine levels. To do this, the user must continue to take the drug. Cocaine overdoses are not uncommon—cocaine can cause fatal strokes, heart attacks, or increases in body temperature (especially if the user is being very physically active at the same time). Long-term use can cause paranoia and hostility, though these seem to disappear when an addict stops using the drug. Other long-term consequences include permanent damage to the heart and to neurons that release serotonin and dopamine, which may result in irreversible mood and movement disorders.

Heroin

Heroin is an opiate, a class of drugs that cause a rush of pleasure followed by a dreamy, carefree state. With opiates, a person is able to feel pain, but the pain seems entirely unimportant. Heroin slows breathing, and can cause vomiting and constipation. In the brain, heroin actually replaces certain neurotransmitters (see page 35), and affects the release of many hormones and other neurotransmitters, with a wide variety of results.

Heroin works with receptors for the endorphin/enkephalin family of neurotransmitters. This family of chemicals controls motion, moods, and body functions such as digestion, temperature, and breathing. It is also quite important in activating the pleasure pathway. Usually, only a few endorphin/enkephalin receptors would be filled, and so there would be only a few such

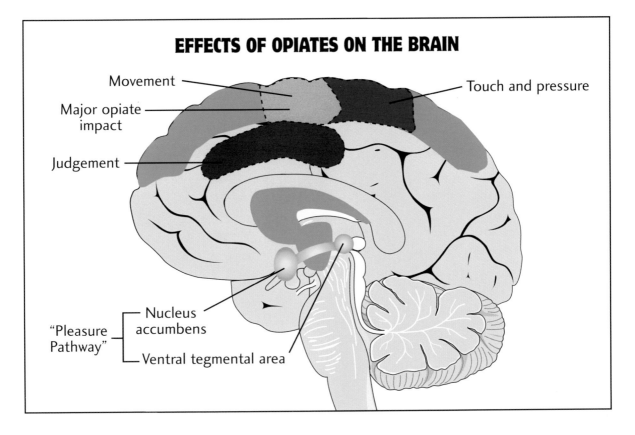

EFFECTS OF OPIATES ON THE BRAIN

Movement
Touch and pressure
Major opiate impact
Judgement
"Pleasure Pathway"
Nucleus accumbens
Ventral tegmental area

neurons firing at any one time. When heroin enters the brain, however, it actually fools the receptors into thinking it is a member of the endorphin/enkephalin family. This means heroin replaces these neurotransmitters and takes their receptors "hostage." The unnatural result is that practically all of the endorphin/enkephalin neurons fire at once.

Fatal overdoses from heroin are not unusual. Death is typically caused by the drug's effect on the breathing centers of the brain. As with any drug purchased illegally, accidental overdoses are common because the concentration of the drug can vary to a wide degree. Likewise, the purity of the drug can also vary—in many cases the drug contains other toxic ingredients.

Despite the highly addictive nature of opiates, they are used widely in medicine as one of the most effective drugs for managing pain.

Marijuana is classified as a narcotic by the U.S. Drug Enforcement Administration.

Marijuana

Marijuana is considered a narcotic by the U.S. Drug Enforcement Administration. Its effects vary widely, but are all typically mild. In general, it causes relaxation and drowsiness, with hallucinations possible, though unlikely. It increases the heart rate slightly and, if smoked, damages the lungs over time the way cigarettes do.

Recent research indicates that THC (tetrahydrocannabinol), the active ingredient in marijuana, causes dopamine levels to rise in the nucleus accumbens, part of the pleasure pathway. Though marijuana is one of the less dangerous drugs in terms of physical damage, it does harm neurons in the hippocampus, which is a critical part of the brain in the formation of new memories. Whether this damage is permanent is unknown. The most dangerous aspects of marijuana use are the changes in sensation and perception, which can cause disorientation and can interfere with a person's ability to react to the environment effectively.

Ecstasy (MDMA)

MDMA (methylenedioxymethamphetamine), known as Ecstasy, is a stimulant. First created in a lab in the 1930s to suppress appetite, it was never tested or marketed. The drug disappeared until the 1980s, when it was briefly and unsuccessfully used in psychotherapy. After this time, the U.S. Drug Enforcement Administration added it to its list of drugs of abuse, and it became popular on the street.

Ecstasy increases heart rate, blood pressure, body temperature, and energy levels. At the same time, it also decreases appetite. The drug is known to cause intense feelings of warm caring and openness in its users—

Ecstasy is a stimulant that raises blood pressure, increases heart rate, and causes a heightened sense of "warmth and caring."

these feelings gave the drug its street name. How Ecstasy works is not fully understood, but in the brain, it seems to increase the amount of dopamine, norepinephrine, and serotonin that is released into synapses. Dopamine helps to activate the pleasure pathway and norepinephrine stimulates some of the heightened physical responses already mentioned (such as increased heart rate). Serotonin, a neurotransmitter much-studied in research on emotion, sleep, and depression, seems to bring about the special effects on mood.

Repeated high doses of MDMA/Ecstasy can cause panic attacks, paranoia, and hallucinations. Researchers are also looking at whether the drug causes long-term damage to—even destruction of—neurons that release serotonin. If so, a likely result for those addicted to this drug would be severe mood disorders, possibly permanent.

Nicotine

Nicotine, the psychoactive ingredient in tobacco, stimulates the heart and blood circulation. Some smokers say nicotine increases their attention and concentration, and in some cases calms them and suppresses appetite, as well.

Nicotine stimulates the nicotinic acetylcholinergic receptors, which are found in neurons throughout the brain. The effect is to increase brain activity in general, particularly in areas involved with memory. When these receptors are blocked in experiments, both people and animals have a hard time remembering new information. So does nicotine actually improve memory? This has not been proven, but researchers are trying to find out if it can help, perhaps in early Alzheimer's disease.

Nicotine is highly addictive, but it does not have the same dangerous mind-altering qualities as some other drugs, such as alcohol or heroin. It can, of course, do serious physical damage with long-term use; smokers are prone to emphysema, lung cancer, heart disease, and even skin damage. People who chew

tobacco are at risk for mouth, lip, and throat cancers, as well as gum disease. In addition, smokers are using a drug that directly affects other people when it is smoked. Secondhand smoke has been shown to be more toxic in some ways than what a smoker breathes in. Secondhand smoke seems to be directly related to lung and heart disease in nonsmokers.

Nicotine is a highly addictive stimulant that increases brain activity.

Chapter

Risks, Signs, and Recovery

There are many things we still don't understand about addiction. One of the biggest questions is why some people are more likely than others to become addicted. Not everyone who experiments with drugs gets hooked, but some people's brains seem to make them especially vulnerable to the changes caused by drug use. These people are the ones most likely to cross over from drug abuse into addiction. Once a person reaches this point, he or she can rarely quit without help.

Who Will Become Addicted?

We cannot predict for certain who will become addicted and who won't, but we do know of some risk factors that may help to determine who is most likely.

One important consideration is the age at which a person first uses a drug. Because a young person's brain, body, and outlook on life are still developing, the risk of addiction is higher for children and teenagers than it is for adults. Compared to most adults, children also have less-developed impulse control. People who start smoking or drinking when they are 15 are many times more likely to have problems with addiction than people who start at age 21 or older. One recent study determined that teenagers can become addicted to nicotine in just a few weeks, even if they only smoke a few cigarettes each day. This is one reason why government agencies try to prevent cigarette advertising that is specifically aimed at teenagers.

Many ads for cigarettes are targeted for young people, who are more likely to become addicted.

Personality is another factor that may affect a person's tendency toward addiction. Today, people believe that "risk-taker" personalities may be more likely than others to experiment with drugs. In the past, experts predicted that obsessive-compulsive personalities were most prone to addiction. Despite many attempts to define the "addictive personality," no one has ever proven precisely what that personality is, or whether one even exists.

Other risk factors and influences are harder to define. They include peer pressure to try or use drugs, and the many influences of home life.

Individual personality and family history are important factors in determining whether addiction will take hold.

Children who grow up in families with substance abusers are much more likely to become substance abusers themselves. This connection seems especially strong for alcoholics. This seems partly due to genetic effects, but it has also been shown to affect people who are not related biologically—for example, members of families with stepparents or adopted children. Part of the risk may also be due to the increased chance of neglect or abuse in these families.

Where to Get Help

The good news is that there is help for people who are addicted. The most important first step is to admit there is a problem. Following is a partial list of places to get help:

- A school counselor
- A doctor or nurse
- A hospital
- Crisis hotlines listed in the community services pages of your phone book
- Yellow pages of the phone book under:
    - Drug Abuse and Addiction—Information and Treatment
    - Smokers' Information and Treatment Centers
    - Alcoholism Information and Treatment Centers
    - Al-Anon/Alateen, *www.al-anon.alateen.org*
    - Cocaine Anonymous, *www.ca.org*
    - Narcotics Anonymous, *www.na.org*
    - National Institute on Drug Abuse, *www.nida.nih.gov*
    - National Drug and Alcohol Treatment Referral Service, 1-800-729-4357

Traumatic or abusive experiences early in life seem to cause actual changes in brain development, not just behavior. When monkeys are neglected or abused as infants, for example, they tend to be overly aggressive and troublesome as adults. If given the opportunity to do so, these abused animals will drink alcohol to excess. These same monkeys have lower than normal levels of the neurotransmitter serotonin in the brain. These changes could also increase the risk of addiction.

Genes Play a Role

Recent research indicates that some people are more likely to become addicted because of a genetic tendency for the brain to generate a positive response to drugs. Several different genes have been linked to nicotine, cocaine, and alcohol addiction. Children of people addicted to these substances have an increased likelihood of addiction themselves.

Does this mean that if you have these genes, you are destined to be a drug addict? Absolutely not. Behavior is a complicated mix of genes, environment, experience, and personal choice. Genetic tendencies don't force people to drink, smoke, or take drugs. They only affect what happens to the neurons after the drug is taken. Many people who have the "alcoholism genes" drink alcohol and do not become addicted. Those genes simply indicate an increased tendency to develop addictive behavior.

Addiction is scary. Will you become addicted to a drug just by trying it? Almost certainly not, although some researchers suspect that "instant addiction" is possible with certain drugs and certain individuals. Addiction almost always grows out of repeated, long-term use—that is certain. How do you make sure you never become addicted? Well, there is only one sure way: it is impossible to become addicted to drugs if you never start using them!

Recognizing Addiction

Someone who uses drugs—even a lot—is not necessarily addicted. The key to recognizing addiction is that the user is no longer in control of the drug use. Very often, an addict will refuse to recognize that there is any problem. This is called denial, and it is very common. Many people who are addicted truly believe that they can quit whenever they want. But people who suffer from true addiction usually cannot quit by themselves. The compulsion to use the drug, driven by the biochemistry of the brain itself, is too strong. This doesn't mean that addiction can't be overcome; many people successfully control addictions. A few unusual people can actually overcome their addictions by themselves, but most people need treatment,

Denial is one major sign of addiction—an addict will refuse to recognize that there is a problem.

including help from family members, friends, and usually a doctor or counselor.

Recovery from addiction can be a long and difficult process. The first—and most important step—is recognizing the problem and affirming a desire to overcome it. To recover, the addict must then give up the one thing that has been the focus of every waking moment.

Withdrawal

The first consequence of giving up a drug is usually withdrawal. Withdrawal is the period during which the body tries to readjust to operating without the drug. Depending on the drug involved, withdrawal can be an intensely painful and unpleasant time for both for the addict and the people who care for him or her.

With drug use, too much dopamine floods the pleasure pathway. You may feel good, but your nerve cells are feverishly working to correct the imbalance. Then, when the drug is gone, the dopamine level can drop too low, and other neurotransmitters also get out of balance. Now you feel dreadful.

Withdrawal can be an intense, uncomfortable experience.

Withdrawal symptoms vary for different drugs, in part depending on the neurotransmitters involved, but they can include nausea, chills, sweating, hallucinations, convulsions, nervousness, anxiety, headaches, depression, extra sensitivity to pain, diarrhea, sleeplessness, and uncontrollable shaking. With

Former First Lady Betty Ford was one of the first high-profile public figures to admit an addiction and to establish ways for people to get help. The Betty Ford Clinic has helped thousands of people with addiction since its founding in Rancho Mirage, California.

certain drugs, withdrawal can even be life-threatening.

An addict who is trying to quit will suffer withdrawal while going through detoxification, which usually lasts for several days to a week. During this time, the addict's body is being weaned completely from the drug. Even after detoxification ends, an addict still has weeks, or even months, of physical and emotional discomfort ahead.

Detoxification usually occurs under medical supervision. Detoxification programs are sometimes tied directly to drug treatment and rehabilitation programs, so once the addicts' bodies are "clean," they have support systems to help keep them that way.

Social Support in Recovery

One of the most important kinds of help an addict can receive is love and support from friends and family. Recovering from addiction requires an addict to re-build self-confidence and to re-learn healthy patterns of living that can replace the old drug-based ones.

Groups such as Alcoholics Anonymous (AA) or Narcotics Anonymous (NA) can provide some of this support. Members of these groups have experienced drug addiction themselves—they know that recovery is hard. They also know that change and new patterns of behavior are possible. Related groups, such as Al-Anon and Alateen, provide support for families and friends of addicts.

support the activity of neurons and repair cells.

Hallucinogens Drugs of abuse that can cause heightened or distorted sensations and perceptions; includes mescaline, PCP, and LSD.

Hypothalamus A part of the brain that is the command center for body temperature, thirst and appetite, sexual behavior, blood pressure, aggression, fear, and sleep. Appears to be important in the pleasure pathway.

Inhibitory Tending to slow or reduce activity.

Limbic system A group of structures in the brain, including the amygdala and nucleus accumbens, that control some basic life functions, manage emotions, and help in memory. Appears to be important in the pleasure pathway.

Narcotics Drugs of abuse that can relieve pain and cause euphoria and drowsiness; includes heroin, codeine, morphine, and other opiates.

Nervous system The brain, spinal cord, and all the nerves in the body.

Neuron A nerve cell, consisting of a cell body, axon, and dendrites.

Neurotransmitter Chemical released from the axon of a neuron that crosses the synaptic cleft to activate another neuron. More generally, any naturally produced chemical that affects the action of the brain or nervous system.

Over-the-counter drug A drug or medication sold in stores with no prescription needed for purchase.

Pleasure pathway An area of the brain believed to be important in learning and remembering positive experiences, which in turn can influence future behavior, including drug addiction. Its specific parts are still being learned, but the limbic system (especially the amygdala and nucleus accumbens), hypothalamus, and brain stem seem to be important.

Psychoactive drug A drug that has effects on the brain.

Receptors Places on a neuron's dendrites that accept neurotransmitters released by the axons of other neurons into the synaptic cleft.

Recovery In addiction, the process of getting and staying off drugs.

Re-uptake The process by which used neurotransmitters are recycled by the axons that released them.

Risk factor An event, attitude, fact, or tendency that makes a person more prone to something (e.g., addiction).

Stimulants Drugs of abuse that can

increase alertness, decrease fatigue, and cause euphoria; includes amphetamines, cocaine, nicotine, and caffeine.

Synapse Junction of the axon of one neuron, a tiny fluid-filled gap called the synaptic cleft, and the receptors on the dendrites of another neuron. Neurotransmitters convey messages from neuron to neuron at the synapse.

Tolerance An aspect of addiction in which, over time, the drug user needs a drug more frequently and in greater quantity to achieve the desired effect.

Withdrawal A phase of addiction in which an addict ceases to use a drug; may be characterized by severe physical and psychological discomfort.

For More Information

BOOKS

Bayer, Linda. *Amphetamines and Other Uppers* (Junior Drug Awareness). New York: Chelsea House Pub., 1999.

Bayer, Linda. *Crack and Cocaine* (Junior Drug Awareness). New York: Chelsea House, 2000.

Brennan, Kristine. *Ecstasy and Other Designer Drugs* (Junior Drug Awareness). New York: Chelsea House Pub., 1999.

Clayton, Lawrence. *Alcohol* (Drug Dangers). Springfield, NJ: Enslow Publishers, Inc., 1999.

Gallagher, Jim. *Heroin* (Drug Dangers). Springfield, NJ: Enslow Publishers, Inc., 1999.

Haughton, Emma. *Drinking, Smoking, and Other Drugs* (Health and Fitness). Chatham, NJ: Raintree/Steck Vaughn, 2000.

Houle, Michelle M. *Tranquilizer, Barbiturate, and Downer* (Drug Dangers). Springfield, NJ: Enslow Publishers, Inc., 2000.

Kozar, Richard. *How to Get Help* (Junior Drug Awareness). New York: Chelsea House Pub., 2000.

Littell, Mary Ann. *Heroin* (Drug Dangers). Springfield, NJ: Enslow Publishers, Inc., 1999.

Monroe, Judy. *Steroid* (Drug Dangers). Springfield, NJ: Enslow Publishers, Inc., 1999.

Peacock, Nancy. *Alcohol* (Junior Drug Awareness). New York: Chelsea House Pub., 2000.

Powell, Jillian. *Why Do People Smoke* (Why Books). Chatham, NJ: Raintree/Steck Vaughn, 2001.

Robbins, Paul R. *Crack and Cocaine* (Drug Dangers). Springfield, NJ: Enslow Publishers, Inc., 1999.

WEB SITES

Close to Home:

Find out the latest scientific advances in understanding and treating addiction— *www.pbs.org/wnet/closetohome/ home.html*

Club Drugs

Learn more about the effects of drugs, such as ecstasy and LSD— *www.clubdrugs.org*

Mind Over Matter: The Brain's Response to Drugs

Read more about how different drugs affect the brain— *www.nida.nih.gov/MOM/TG/mo mtg-index.html*

Office of National Drug Control Policy

Learn more about what the government is doing to prevent drug abuse— *www.whitehousedrugpolicy.org*

Index

616.86   Papa, Susan.
PAP
         Addiction

2994

616.86   Papa, Susan.
PAP
         Addiction